MY FAVORITE ANIMALS ABC

What's your favorite animal?

By Elizabeth M Helmkamp
Published on Amazon.com

ISBN: 978-1-7361364-2-3
Copyright Date: 1/05/2021
Created in Elmhurst, IL ,USA

Illustrations, cover, and layout designed by Elizabeth M Helmkamp
Created on Android Autodesk Sketchbook, edited with Photoshop

Praise to the Lord,
who made all these amazing creatures!

Dedicated to:
my teachers and family
who encouraged me in my love
of God's creation,

and Kristi:
Hello Kristi. ♡

Hello to you, and welcome all!
Let's meet some new friends big and small!
Some you might have met before
Others hail from a distant shore.

A puzzle for an eager mind:
If you have sharp eyes you will find
the letter that the poem's about.
It's hidden in each scene no doubt!

A is for Albatross

The albatross can glide and glide,
his wingspan measures ten feet wide.
He rarely perches in a tree
and spends his life out on the sea.

B is for Bombardier Beetle

Black and yellow like a bee,
colors that say, "Don't mess with me!"
If those mean ants don't give him room
He'll send them packing with a boom!

C is for Cassowary

Here we meet the cassowary,
a bird that's known for being scary.
Between their claws and drumming roars
they seem to think they're dinosaurs.

D is for Discus

The calm gem of the Amazon
makes milk-like food to feed her spawn,
but they're not mammals, they are fish
round as their name, thin as a dish.

E is for Earthworm

They crawl along and eat debris,
they help the garden grow you see.
Their mouth so small they can't fit teeth
and so they gum along beneath.

F is for Firefly

Each firefly has it's own light,
to find each other in the night.
If you see him glowing yellow
That means he's a friendly fellow.

G is for Gecko

This reptile is called a gecko,
it's different in two ways I'll show:
first, unlike most lizards it sings
and to ceiling or wall it clings.

H is for Honey-badger

Honey-badger is big and long,
to open hives his claws are strong.
And when the bees their honey hide
he gets some help from honey-guide.

I is for Iguana

Found in most any habitat,
eats fruits, leaves, flowers, stuff like that.
The iguana's idea of fun
seems to be basking in the sun.

J is for Jellyfish

In the sea floats the jellyfish,
it stings and grabs food with a swish.
They're big, they're small, they sometimes glow
A group is called a smack, you know!

K is for Komodo dragon

This dragon does not fly or roar,
but hunting is an easy chore.
Her mouth's so gross one bite and lick
is all it takes to make prey sick.

L is for Lacewing

The grown-ups pollinate flowers,
the babies eat aphids for hours.
What do they stand their eggs upon?
Cosmos, dill, and dandelion.

M is for Manta Ray

Their fins can reach twenty three feet,
but zooplankton is what they eat!
They never lay an egg they say -
some types stay put while others stray.

N is for Nightingale

While other birds sing in daylight,
this one instead will sing all night.
It's much easier to be heard
when you're the only singing bird.

O is for Okapi

The okapi is very shy
it rarely sees the open sky.
Stripes of zebra, neck of giraffe
this odd creature is half and half.

P is for Praying Mantis

The patient praying mantis wait,
they are alert. though look sedate.
Something comes by, grab the food quick!
Not food? Pretend to be a stick!

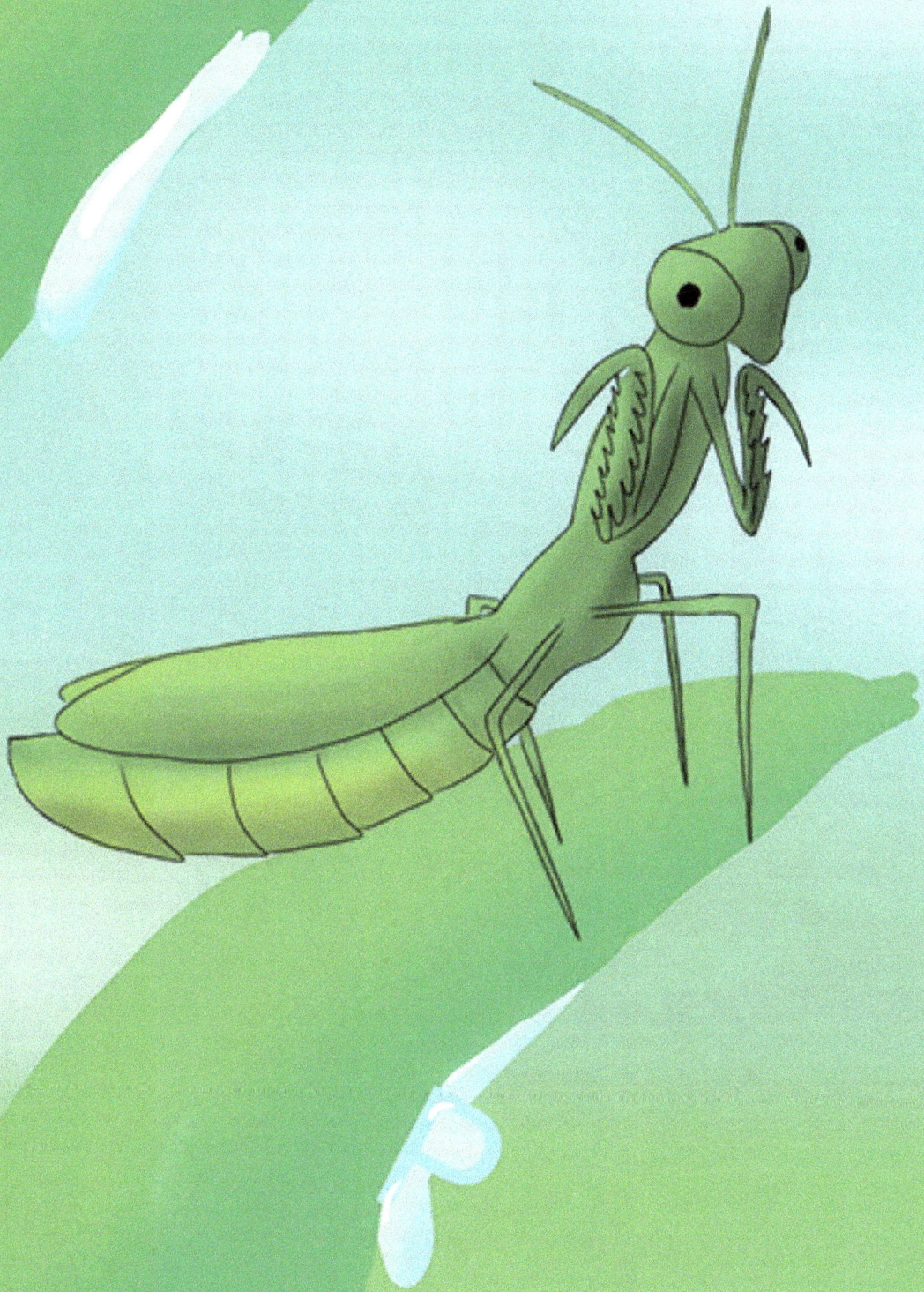

Q is for Quetzal

These colorful shiny quetzal
make their home in rainforests tall.
You can tell which one is the dad
by the long tail in which he's clad.

R is for Raccoon

Raccoons appear to wear a mask,
their thumbs are tools for any task.
They use their heads to find a treat
and wash their paws before they eat.

S is for Salamander

The quick, shiny salamander
in groups to puddles meander.
So many colors and sizes
you'd think they're wearing disguises.

T is for Tetra

Lives in the muddy Amazon,
together to great schools they're drawn.
Colored iridescent in light
their colors fade in dark of night.

U is for Umbrellabird

What this bird lacks in vibrant hue
it makes up for in it's hairdo.
There's just one question on my brain:
Does it truly block the rain?

V is for Vole

He looks like a fat short-tailed mouse,
but you won't find him in a house.
They like to eat both bark and root -
their friends are friends for life, how cute!

W is for Weasel

The tricky weasel likes to prance,
confusing rabbits with its dance.
Fits in most tunnels to be sure -
when seasons change so does their fur.

X is for Xenopus

Xenopus aren't like most frogs
who sit and catch flies on their logs.
Who needs a tougue and who needs teeth
with little claws upon your feet?

Y is for Yabby

The yabby crayfish likes to roam,
Australia's where they make their home.
From black to brown to vibrant blue
the river's health decides their hue.

Z is for Zebra

Why does a zebra wear such stripes?
Zebras are not the hiding types.
Some say they help him cool and heat
or confuse lions trying to eat.

Why the Albatross is Awesome!

Albatrosses have the largest wing and life span of any living bird. Most of the 21 species live over 50 years and their wingspans range from 5.7-12 ft, with a 10 foot average. To compare: the heaviest bird, the condor, has a maximum wingspan of 10.5 feet. The albatross is built for flying incredibly long distances. To save energy on the journey, they have mastered gliding on the wind. Albatross wings even lock in place so they don't get tired holding them open! They are so efficient at flying that their heart rate while flying is the same as while they are resting!

Why the Bombardier Beetle is the Best!

These beetles can be found on every continent except Antarctica! Bombardiers eat and act like regular beetles, except for their extraordinary defense mechanism. The beetle stores hydroquinone and hydrogen peroxide in two separate pouches in its abdomen. These chemicals each are toxic on their own, but when combined they create a chemical reaction that produces enough heat to instantly boil the chemicals and produce a loud explosion of heat and toxic gas. They themselves are immune to the chemicals, and don't even get burned by the 212ºF explosion! These little gunners are truly incredible!

Why the Cassowary is Cool!

Cassowaries are a keystone species in rainforests in New Guinea and other nearby islands. They are often called "dinosaur birds" because their skeleton is similar to that of a velociraptor. While they hunt opportunistically, the cassowary is actually an omnivore and plays a major role in the dispersal of seeds. During mating they make a drumming call to mark their territory. Cassowaries are very teritorial, even attacking humans who get too close. One of the most dangerous traits of this bird is it's daggerlike second claw, which it uses as a weapon. They can run up to 50 mph, swim, and even kick down small trees. This is truly a wild bird!

Why the Discus is Dazzling!

Discus are a rather unique type of cichlid (pronounced: si-kluhd). Unlike most cichlids, discus travel in groups and they eat more plants than other types of cichlid. When it comes time to raise their young (called fry) they pair off away from the group and stay by them for the first two weeks. During this time they produce a mucus to feed the fry, much like milk in mammals. After that they wean the fry to teach them how to find food. It takes four weeks until the fry can live on their own. What beautiful and gentle creatures!

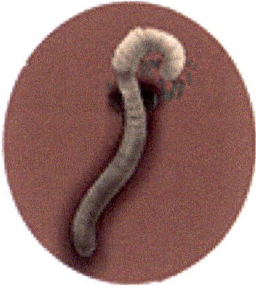

Why Earthworms are Electrifying!

Earthworms are important to soil health in many ways. They create a fertile mixture of dead plants and soil called humus. Earthworms have no teeth, and so they eat dirt and sand to grind food in the gizzard. By creating burrows they mix and aerate the soil. Earthworm bodies are divided into segments and they move by expanding and contracting these segments in waves along their body. Most can regenerate damaged or missing segments, but it depends on the species how much they can regenerate. Some can regenerate two worms from being cut in half. These soil creatures are vital and fascinating parts of our world!

Why Fireflies are Fantastic!

Fireflies, sometimes called lightning bugs, can often be seen glowing by the hundreds in grassy fields on summer evenings. Most species feed on pollen, and glow various shades of yellow. Though rare, there are also blue and green fireflies. As I found out the hard way, the green ones (photuris fireflies) actually eat other species of firefly by mimicking their signals. So, if you want to see an awesome show of bioluminescence up close and in action by catching and releasing them, remember yellow is a friendly fellow!

Why Geckos are Great!

Geckos are most well known for, of course, the adhesive pads on their feet that allow them to cling to any surface at any angle using what is basically static electricity. However this is far from the only unique thing! Like mentioned in the poem, geckos have vocal cords used to make various chirping noises. They do this to warn others of danger, establish territory, or attract a mate. To keep their eyes moist they lick their own eyes! When there is no male around, females will lay eggs that clone themselves instead of having regular eggs. These strange and fascinating creatures are truly great!

Why Honey-badgers are Hip!

The honey-badger is actually not a badger! It is the only species in its genus and more closely resembles martins. Their hind claws are short, while their front claws are long for tearing into beehives and digging. Honey-badger's favorite foods are snakes, (including the deadly black mamba) and bees, but it can eat many things. They often find honey on their own, but honey-guides will sometimes join them for a meal. While studies are unclear who is following whom, honey-guides are known to guide people to beehives, behavior thought to have been brought over from their relationship with the honey-badger.

Why Iguanas are Impressive!

Iguanas are the quintessential lizards. Scaly and peaceful, these lizards are found in many habitats. There are both land and marine iguanas! One of the identifying features of iguanas are the large spikes that go down their backs. Like most reptiles iguanas are cold blooded and rely on external temperatures to regulate their internal body temperature. As a result, you can often find them sunning themselves on rocks.

Why Jellyfish are Jolly!

Jellyfish can be used to refer to any animal in the subphylum Medusozoa but "true jellyfish" all belong to the class Scyphozoa. To be fair, that's still a lot of species. Jellyfish come in all colors and sizes, and all of them are beautiful. They are found near coasts all over the world! All true Scyphozoa jellyfish live in saltwater, but there are other species of "freshwater jellyfish" that exist in parts of the world. Several species of jellyfish produce bioluminescent proteins that glow in the dark. All of them have round bells for their heads and stinging tentacles that they use to capture their food.

Why Komodo Dragons are Kingly!

Komodo dragons are a large type of monitor lizard. They live on a few Indonesian islands: Rinca Island, Flores Island, Gili Montang Island, and Komodo Island from where they get their name. Komodos are solitary creatures who live in burrows. One of the most interesting things about komodo dragons is their saliva. While they have a venom, it is only an anticoagulant which prevents wounds from healing. The true deadly force of their bite comes from the bacteria in their mouths, which causes prey to die of an infection. Sitting at the top of the food chain in the islands where they live, they are truly kingly!

Why Lacewings are Legendary!

Lacewings are insects in the family Chrysopidae. Like many insects, they have four distinct life stages. The eggs are laid on slender stalks that keep them off the surface of the leaf. The larvae resemble tiny alligators and eat constantly, sucking dry 30-50 aphids per day. They cover themselves with the dead husks for camouflage. After three or four weeks they make cocoons and become pupa. The adult lacewings become pollinators when they emerge, and lay up to a hundred eggs on their favorite plants like cosmos, dill, sunflower, carrots or dandelions. Farmers and gardeners value them highly as both a natural pest control and helpful pollinators.

Why Manta Rays are Magnificent!

There are two species of manta ray. Both are found in warm waters. The manta M. Birostris reaches 23 ft wide and migrates long distances. The manta M. Alfredi reaches 18 ft and stays near it's home coast. Both species give live birth. These gentle giants are filter feeders, eating microscopic particles called zooplankton as they swim along. The name "manta" is Portuguese and Spanish for "mantle" or "cloak" or "blanket". Much like whales, they are known to breach, or leap from the water. They hunt in packs, surrounding plankton and swirling it into a tight ball that they can dive through. These beautiful and clever giants are truly magnificent!

Why Nightingales are Neat!

The nightingale is a nocturnal flycatcher known for it's beautiful nighttime song. Its name literally means "night singer". They are native to Europe, Africa, and Asia Minor. Slightly larger than the average robin, the nightingale's plain brown plumage doesn't make it a particularly eye catching bird. However, it's song is a fine example of how one should never judge by appearances. The nightingale's song has an impressive range of notes and noises, and is most easily recognized by a whistling crescendo. They sing at night and dawn. At night they sing to attract a mate. At dawn they sing with other birds to keep their territory safe. Nightingales are truly unique birds!

Why Okapis are Out of This World!

The okapi has long been my personal favorite animal. Despite being striped like a zebra, they are the only living relative of the giraffe. They live in the Ituri rain-forest of Africa. They may not look super camouflaged based on a picture, but in the wild they are very difficult to spot. Even at the zoo it is easy to stare right at an okapi and miss it! Their fur is purplish to reddish brown or black, and waterproof from the oils in it. Their rump stripes are called "follow me stripes" because they help a baby okapi stay with its mom. They make calls, but they are too deep for most predators, and us, to hear. Okapis keep to themselves, so they were not discovered until 1900! Today there are estimated to be about 25,000 in the wild. These mysterious animals are fascinating!

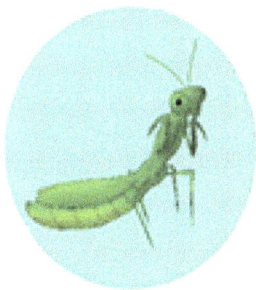

Why Praying Mantises are Precious!

Praying mantises are ambush predators and will stay in one place for long periods of time as long as they are well fed in that spot. Their front legs are not used for walking but instead are used like hands, making them look vaguely like a centaur. They are masters of camoflauge by blending in to the background, or even pretending to be a flower. Some can even turn black after a forest fire to blend in better! Like the walking stick, the praying mantis will sway side to side when threatened, imitating a stick in the breeze and allowing it to get a better look at the potential threat. If this doesn't work, the manits will bluff, spreading its wings and claws to make itself look scary.

Why Quetzals are Queenly!

Quetzals (kwet·zlz) (singular: kuht·saal) are brightly colored birds from rain-forests and humid highlands in South and Central America. They eat fruits, berries, and insects. Quetzals disperse the seeds of the avocado by swallowing the pits whole and regurgitating the seeds! The name translates to "large brilliant tail feather" from the Nahuatl language. The males are known for these long tail feathers, which reach about 26 inches long. The birds themselves are 16 inches long. Dads do the daytime egg sitting, moms sit at night. Fathers lay their tail feathers out of the tree cavity to disguise the nest as a fern!

Why Raccoons are Rad!

Raccoons are common sights in urban and forested areas. These animals are highly adaptable and intelligent. They have a very strong sense of touch, but their paws have a tough covering which becomes soft when wet! As a result they will "wash" their food, but in fact they are getting it wet to better feel it. They also have a keen sense of hearing to locate tasty earthworms while their eyes are not so great as they are colorblind. Intelligence studies have shown that they are able to solve complex puzzles and remember solutions for three years. They are omnivores, and eat about even amounts meat and fruit. Individual raccoons even have favorite foods!

Why Salamanders are Swell!

There are many species of salamanders all over the world. All salamanders are amphibians. Some spend most of their lives on land, some switch between the water and land, and others never leave the water. Some salamanders that don't leave the water, such as sirens, do not have hind limbs, but most have four legs. Many species have a prehensile tail, which helps it climb trees. Other species have a flat tail for swimming. Some have gills, others have lungs, still others breathe through their skin. All baby salamanders breath through gills and are aquatic. Some are brightly colored to tell predators they taste bad, while others blend right in!

Why Tetras are Terrific!

In the wild of the Amazon, tetra coloration is red and blue striped and they are easy to spot. Tetras are most well known as a popular aquarium fish. Because of their popularity in captivity, little is known about them in the wild. Their coloration is iridescent rather than pigment based, so their colors change based on the light. The reason for their bright coloration is unknown! As pets, they have been bred to have many other patterns. They eat mostly insect larvae, algae, and microscopic creatures. They are known to be highly social and travel in schools. How terrific to see a tetra!

Why Umbrellabirds are Ultra!

Umbrellabirds are found in Central and South American rain-forests. Despite their monochromatic black feathers, they are easily recognizable by their umbrella shaped crest and long wattle. The wattle hanging down the front is inflatable and meant to amplify their booming calls. The male umbrellabirds gather in groups and display their calls and wattles, competing for the attention of the females. The females will then raise the chicks on their own. They are not known for their good nest building skills as their nests are flimsy. They mostly eat plants, but will eat lizards occasionally. Ultimately, these umbrellabirds are unique!

Why Voles are Valiant!

Voles are often confused with mice but are different in that they are rounder and have a shorter tail. Voles are common pests, and are known to eat the bark of small trees and cut paths in grass to find their other favorite food: roots. Sadly, eating the roots often kills the plant. Because of this diet, they are not often found in houses. Voles even pick one mate to stay with for life, and are somewhat social. Studies have shown that voles are capable of empathy, and will groom hurt or mistreated members more than others. This was previously thought to be something only highly intelligent creatures were capable of, like elephants and apes. Even though voles eat garden plants, they seem valiant!

Why Weasels are Winsome!

The term weasel originally only referred to what is now known as the least weasel, but now refers to any species of stoat, ferret, polecat, etc, in the Mustela genus. Weasels generally have brown coats with white bellies in summer, and in places with snowy winters they tend to turn white as temperatures fall. All weasels eat rodents and birds, as they are able to follow their prey into tiny burrows! An interesting phenomenon that weasels are known for is the weasel war dance. When the weasel is excited, particularly when hunting, they will begin a series of reckless hops and flips while making a popping or clucking noise often pronounced, "Dook dook". This is used to disorient prey though in domestic species such as ferrets it's also a sign of happiness! How winsome and friendly!

Why Xenopus are X-elent!

Xenopus live in ponds most of the year. They rarely leave the water unless forced out. When the water dries up they bury themselves in the mud and wait. All twenty species live in the lower half of Africa. Xenopus have no teeth, tongues, vocal sacs, eyelids, or eardrums. This leads to their rather silly look. Because xenopus have no vocal sacks they can't croak, so they make clicking noises instead. Their feet are webbed and on each foot there are only three claws. They are scavengers and use their claws to find and "chew" food. They are often used in research about how to cure birth defects or cancer due to their easy to work with genetics.

Why Yabbies Make Us Say Yahoo!

Yabbies are a sort of crayfish that lives in Australia. Their burrows are made in riverbanks and dams. When water is clear their shell colors range from dark brown to dark blue to black. When the water is muddy or cloudy their colors can be tan or greenish brown. They will migrate up to 37 miles to find new or better water! When temperatures drop or during drought, they hibernate in their burrows. Yabbies are detrivores, meaning they eat dead or decaying plants and animals. They mostly search for these at night, and sleep during the day. Yabbies are a popular food, though hunting is limited because they are listed as vulnerable. No hook is needed to catch them. People simply tie meat to a string and they won't let it go!

Why Zebras are Zany!

Zebras are a popular animal at the zoo and in many animal books, and for good reason. While many animals have smooth, even coloring, scientists have debated the zebra's eye catching stripes for years! There are 18 different theories about why they have stripes! The three most popular theories are: heat regulation, confusing predators, and protection from flies. The ideas behind the stripes protecting from predators and flies are similar: they both rely on the fact that as the zebra moves the stripes confuse the vision of the attacker. Regulating heat is thought to work by raising the fur in the black stripes to trap heat and lowering it to allow sweat to evaporate faster. The white stripes reflect, creating airflow to spread the effects. Either way they look really neat!

Works Cited

"Albatross."Wikipedia, 31 Oct. 2020, en.wikipedia.org/wiki/Albatross#Breeding_and_dancing. Accessed 18 Nov. 2020.

"Bombardier Beetle." Wikipedia, 5 Nov. 2020, en.wikipedia.org/wiki/Bombardier_beetle.

Bull, J. J., et al. "Deathly Drool: Evolutionary and Ecological Basis of Septic Bacteria in Komodo Dragon Mouths." PLoS ONE, vol. 5, no. 6, 21 June 2010, p. e11097, 10.1371/journal.pone.0011097. Accessed 24 Sept. 2020.

"Cardinal Tetra." Wikipedia, 27 Sept. 2020, en.wikipedia.org/wiki/Cardinal_tetra. Accessed 24 Nov. 2020.

"Common Yabby." Wikipedia, 20 Oct. 2020, en.wikipedia.org/wiki/Common_yabby#cite_note-4. Accessed 30 Nov. 2020.

"Earthworm." Wikipedia, 25 June 2020, en.wikipedia.org/wiki/Earthworm.

Executive, Digital. "StackPath." Jungletours.com.Au, 1 Feb. 2019, jungletours.com.au/is-a-cassowary-a-dinosaur/. Accessed 18 Nov. 2020.

Law, Yao-Hua. "The Truth behind Why Zebras Have Stripes." Www.Bbc.com, 11 Dec. 2019, www.bbc.com/future/article/20191031-the-truth-behind-why-zebras-have-stripes.Works Cited

"Leopard Gecko | San Diego Zoo Animals & Plants." Sandiegozoo.org, 2020, animals.sandiegozoo.org/animals/leopard-gecko.

Nargi, Lela. "Scientists Solve Mystery of Bombardier Beetles' Hot, Toxic Spray." Washington Post, www.washingtonpost.com/lifestyle/kidspost/scientists-solve-mystery-ofbombardier-beetles-hot-toxic-spray/2020/07/02/b0149ea4-badd-11ea-bdaf-a129f921026f_story.html. Accessed 18 Nov. 2020. Accessed 23 Sept.

OISAT. "Lacewing." Www.Oisat.org, PAN Germany, www.oisat.org/control_methods/natural_enemies/predators/lacewing.html. Accessed 24 Nov. 2020.

"Okapi | San Diego Zoo Animals & Plants." Sandiegozoo.org, 2019, animals.sandiegozoo.org/animals/okapi.

"Salamander." Wikipedia, 23 Nov. 2020, en.wikipedia.org/wiki/Salamander. Accessed 24 Nov. 2020.

"The Honey Badger - Associations." Www.Honeybadger.com, www.honeybadger.com/associations.html. Accessed 20 Nov. 2020.

"Types of Fireflies." Firefly.org, www.firefly.org/types-of-fireflies.html. Accessed 19 Nov. 2020.

"Umbrellabird." Wikipedia, 13 Feb. 2020, en.wikipedia.org/wiki/Umbrellabird. Accessed 24 Nov. 2020.

"Vole." Wikipedia, 29 Nov. 2020, en.wikipedia.org/wiki/Vole. Accessed 30 Nov. 2020.

"Weasel." Wikipedia, 26 Nov. 2020, en.wikipedia.org/wiki/Weasel. Accessed 30 Nov. 2020.

"Weasel War Dance." Wikipedia, 16 Mar. 2020, en.wikipedia.org/wiki/Weasel_war_dance. Accessed 30 Nov 2020.

Wikipedia Contributors. "Cassowary." Wikipedia, Wikimedia Foundation, 5 Apr. 2019, en.wikipedia.org/wiki/Cassowary.

---. "Common Nightingale." Wikipedia, Wikimedia Foundation, 24 Nov. 2019, en.wikipedia.org/wiki/Common_nightingale.

---. "Discus (Fish)." Wikipedia, Wikimedia Foundation, 18 Sept. 2019, en.wikipedia.org/wiki/Discus_(fish). Accessed 23 Sept. 2019.

---. "Gecko." Wikipedia, Wikimedia Foundation, 10 Jan. 2019, en.wikipedia.org/wiki/Gecko.

---. "Honey Badger." Wikipedia, Wikimedia Foundation, 25 Oct. 2019, en.wikipedia.org/wiki/Honey_badger

---. "Iguana." Wikipedia, Wikimedia Foundation, 18 Mar. 2019, en.wikipedia.org/wiki/Iguana.

---. "Jellyfish." Wikipedia, Wikimedia Foundation, 21 Feb. 2019, en.wikipedia.org/wiki/Jellyfish.

---. "Komodo Dragon." Wikipedia, Wikimedia Foundation, 8 Apr. 2019, en.wikipedia.org/wiki/Komodo_dragon.

---. "Manta Ray." Wikipedia, Wikimedia Foundation, 4 Apr. 2019, en.wikipedia.org/wiki/Manta_ray.

---. "Mantis." Wikipedia, Wikimedia Foundation, 19 Apr. 2019, en.wikipedia.org/wiki/Mantis.

---. "Raccoon." Wikipedia, Wikimedia Foundation, 29 Apr. 2019, en.wikipedia.org/wiki/Raccoon.

---. "Resplendent Quetzal." Wikipedia, Wikimedia Foundation, 31 Dec. 2018, en.wikipedia.org/wiki/Resplendent_Quetzal. Accessed 7 Feb. 2019.

"Xenopus." Wikipedia, 9 Nov. 2020, en.wikipedia.org/wiki/Xenopus. Accessed 30 Nov. 2020. animals.sandiegozoo.org/animals/leopard-gecko.

www.ingramcontent.com/pod-product-compliance
Lightning Source LLC
Chambersburg PA
CBHW041602260326
41914CB00011B/1364